Stories From My Father

Barbara Paulding

Published by Happy Jack Publishing, LLC

Copyright © April 2014
by Barbara Paulding

First Printing April 2014

ISBN-10: 0615999158
ISBN-13: 978-0615999159

DEDICATION

This book is dedicated to my great grandpa, Jacob and my grandpa, John. Thank you for joining the early fight for workers' rights and for helping our family embrace the union values of equality and fraternity.

ACKNOWLEDGMENTS

I want to say a special thank you to Happy Jack Publishing and to my editor, Beth Burgmeyer. Her expertise and dedication have made this a very rewarding and exciting endeavor.

Finally, thank you to all of the union men and women who continue to work tirelessly for workers' rights and equality.

PROLOGUE

The story of the Pauldings is a story of coal miners, families and the dirt and dust of southern Iowa. Although there were many coal mining towns in southern Iowa, my dad's story is inexorably bound to the little coal mining town of Hamilton, Iowa. Hamilton cradled him in infancy, watched over him as he grew, and was always home, a place to return to.

From 1911 until 2012, the lots that my grandfather bought were owned and cared for by someone in the family. Throughout the years, Hamilton remained my dad's favorite place to go. Even when he was one hundred years old, he usually got out of the car and sat in the yard for a while. Dad loved to take his lawn chair and sit under the trees, the same trees he had played under as a child.

Just before Dad died, we took one of our weekly drives to Hamilton. It was a misty March day, and as we drove slowly through Hamilton, Dad delighted in showing me where the pool hall, grocery store, and union hall used to be. We ended up at the Methodist church where he had spent so much of his childhood. That was his last trip to the little mining town he loved.

I am very grateful that my dad was a prolific storyteller. Because of the stories my father told me, his family's rich history is still alive. I have all of the memories and some of the pictures. I hope I have been able to preserve some sense of the people and the places my Dad knew and loved.

THE BEGINNING

The baby is born on a cold rainy day in April in the year of our Lord 1909 in Hootie, Illinois. He isn't born in a hospital or a gracious home, with doctors and nurses in attendance.

He is born in a coal miners shack, attended at his birth by a midwife and his four older brothers and sisters.

If you have never been in a coal miner's shack it will be hard for you to picture his birthplace. Let me try to set the stage for you.

Coal miner's shacks, also known as camp houses, are owned by the big mining companies and are rented out to the miners who work in their mines. They are cheap, clapboard affairs, frequently covered only in black tar paper. The tar paper siding, the porous windows and doors, make it difficult for the families who live in them to stay warm in the winter. But there are some important amenities. Every camp house has a big coal stove in the main room. The stove fights hard to push back against the freezing weather. Each kitchen has a wood cook stove, which not only cooks the family's meals, but also helps to keep the house warm.

When you come through the back door of the baby's birthplace, the first thing you notice is the big wood stove. The day the baby is born, that stove is filled with brightly burning wood and the reservoir is filled with hot water. There is also a special place behind the stove that has been cleared of the many boots and coats that are usually piled there to dry. This is where the midwife will place the baby's box. This is where the baby will sleep for the first few weeks of his life. The big stove will help to keep him warm.

The kitchen floor is made of simple wooden planks and the splinters that are ever present in the rough wood continuously plague little feet. All of the cracks in the floor are filled with coal dust. The room is poorly lit. In the evening the only source of light will be the kerosene lamp that sits in the middle of the simple wooden table. The table and chairs are the only furnishings in the room.

Ida Paulding, the baby's mother, is in one of the bedrooms off of the kitchen. The midwife comes to the kitchen, dips hot water out of the reservoir and returns to the bedroom. The baby's brothers and sisters huddle together in the kitchen, waiting, expectant. Two year old Nellie cries for her mama. Then they hear it. A small cry, a baby's wail.

The midwife returns to the kitchen, carrying a little bundle. She looks at the other children, the shabby but clean camp house, and shakes her head. *"Coal miners,"* she mutters under her breath. She goes behind the stove and gently places the baby in the little box. *"Now you children leave your brother alone,"* she says sternly.

As soon as she leaves the room, the children crowd behind the stove to look at this new little person. He is fast asleep. Little Nellie pokes him in the belly and he opens his eyes, stares up at his brothers and sisters and starts to cry.

Later, the children are allowed to see their mother.

"What'll we call him, Ma?" eight year old Faye asks.

Ida pushes the hair off of her forehead and shakes her head. *"I don't know, child, I just don't know."*

The baby does not have a name for three weeks. Ida is just too tired to care. Faye starts calling the baby Jim Crow, a reflection of the times. When the baby's father, John, hears Faye crooning to him, calling him Little Jimmy Crow, John decides it is time the baby had a proper name. John sits his daughter down and talks to her. His message is a simple one. *"Faye, I really like the name Jimmy. Let's keep that name, but you have to drop the word 'crow.' We can't use that name in this house. I'm union and the union stand for equality. The word Jim Crow is not about equality, understand?"*

Fays nods her head, even though she doesn't understand a word he has said about equality. Nevertheless, she does as her father says and drops the word Crow from the little baby's name. The baby finally has a name: Jimmy Paulding.

THE MOVE

In March, 1911, Jimmy's parents decide to leave all of their friends and family and move to Hamilton, Iowa.

On the day of the move there is a new baby in the box behind the cook stove. The baby is Jimmy's little sister, Ethyl. The camp house is strangely quiet that day. All of the furniture has been sold. The children are dressed in their best clothes. Ida and John gather them up, take the baby out of the box and herd them out to the wagon that is waiting to take them to the train. John's brothers, Shorty and Lou, join them. They too are ready for a new life, a new beginning.

This has not been an easy decision for John to make. He is close to his father, Jacob, and wonders when he will ever see him again. He worries about the jobs the union men have been telling people about. Is it true? Are there really that many mining jobs in Hamilton? But he has faith in the union, so he leaves his home in search of a better life.

When the Paulding family arrives at the train station in Hamilton, it is apparent to John that all of the stories about jobs are true. The town is booming. There are people everywhere. Women and children are strolling down the dusty streets. There are rows and rows of new camp houses.

Hamilton Main Street

The Paulding family is assigned to one of the new camp houses. Every camp house has a big coal stove in the parlor, a big kitchen, three bedrooms and a nice front porch that spans the length of the house. The new wooden floors have splinters but there is no coal dust embedded in the cracks. The yard is full of promise. With spring rains, the grass will turn green, the big oak trees will leaf out and John will plant a life giving garden.

The Paulding home stands on C Street, next to the post office. Just down the street there is a pool hall, grocery store, payroll office and union hall. Several blocks over, there is a white clapboard Methodist Church and a two story school house.

Hamilton Church

Hamilton School

John digs up part of the yard for a garden. He and Shorty go to work in the mines. There are many mines around Hamilton, one of the biggest is the Golden Goose. John and Shorty both work there for a long time. Lou decides to go to Des Moines. He moves fifty miles from his brothers to seek a different future.

Golden Goose Mine

Ida goes to work too, trying to make the camp house a home. She cleans, cooks and keeps the children corralled. Every Saturday night she bathes all of the children, one at a time, in the wash tub. Every Sunday she dresses all six of them in clean clothes, slicks down their hair, and takes them to the Methodist church.

Jimmy by the Methodist Church

In the fall, when school starts, all of the children who are old enough, march to school in clean clothes and slicked down hair. Ida feels a sense of peace, of hope. Her children will have a chance here, to learn and to know God.

It is a hard life, but Ida is determined that things will be good here for the six little bundles she pushed out of her body in Hootie, Illinois.

JIMMY'S PARENTS

Ida McClure Paulding & John Paulding

Children's memories of their parents give us a snapshot, a mirror into what their life seemed like to the little people they raised.

I have always found it interesting, the picture I have of my grandpa and grandma from listening to the stories told by my dad and his brothers and sisters.

Although no one ever tried to sugarcoat the fact that John Paulding was a payday drunk, that he terrorized his family when he was drunk, the children all seemed to love him. When I listened to their stories, I knew they were all proud of their father. There were memories of love, of Christmas's made special and of a dad who read them Bible stories. Their memories were mostly memories of the good dad, the good John Paulding. Nellie seemed to sum it all up when she said, *"He was a good dad. He loved us."*

Their stories about Ida Paulding were very different. They really loved and admired their ma. But their stories about their ma were usually about how hard she worked, how good she was, and how she kept the house and all of them clean. There were few anecdotes about love or hugs or bedtime stories. And yet they all knew in some deep, fundamental way, how very much she did love them.

JIMMY'S FATHER, JOHN PAULDING

John Paulding

When he first goes down in the coal mines of Illinois, John Paulding is a seventeen year old boy. He works beside his father, Jacob Paulding. Jacob works in the mines his entire life and is a member of the Progressive Miners Movement, a precursor to the United Mine Workers Union. John becomes a man in the mines. He is physically well suited to the work: short, strong, intelligent and knows instinctively how to shore up a room.

He joins the union, pays his dues and goes out on strike when one is called. It is a hard, dangerous way to live but he feels a certain pride in his abilities, in being brave enough to go into the darkness of the mine. When he marries, and his family grows, he is always able to provide for them. They always have food.

As the years pass, John finds that other miners come to him for advice. He becomes a fierce advocate for workers' rights and equality.

When John L. Lewis becomes the head of the United Mine Workers Union, John believes they finally have a real champion of workers' rights. John L Lewis' picture appears in the house. John tells the children about him: how he fights for workers' rights, mine safety and tries to end the practice of paying the miners in script instead of money.

John L. Lewis   Source: The World's Work

Fighting to get the mine owners to pay the miners' wages in real money instead of script is one of the main battles the union wages against the mine owners. When the miners are paid in script they can only spend their wages at the company store. Getting "real wages" gives the miners a lot more freedom from the mine owners. John is very proud when the union wins this fight.

John's life as a coal miner and union advocate certainly shapes his world outlook and has a direct bearing on his role in the family. As a result of his beliefs, his children all hear a strong, consistent message about equality. This message runs contrary to everything the children see around them. In Hamilton, and many of the surrounding towns, there are signs that proudly proclaim: NO NIGGERS ALLOWED AFTER DARK. The slingshots that Jimmy and his brothers play with are called Nigger Shooters.

The only town near Hamilton that does not have these signs is Buxton. Unlike the other southern Iowa towns, Buxton (a town of 5,000 people) is made up of a majority of African Americans. While there are many professional African Americans living in Buxton (doctors, lawyers, clergy, teachers, and shop keepers) the majority of the men are coal miners and they all belong to the union. When they work in the mines, the African American men are treated equally, receiving equal pay for equal work.

John's fierce adherence to the union's notions of equality is really tested one year when Jimmy is about ten. A strike is called and this time the union and the mine owners are not able to come to any agreement. The strike drags on and on and families get scared. When the men start worrying about feeding their families, not many of them care about the union and equality. John Paulding sometimes feels like he is standing alone.

When the strike is finally settled, the miners are supposed to go back to work according to a strict schedule based on seniority, and the length of time they've been laid off. John is one of the union leaders in charge of getting the men back to work. Some of the white miners threaten John and tell him to *"put the white miners back to work before any of those niggers touch a pick ax again."* Ida is from the south and agrees with the white miners and the Klan. She can't understand John. Jimmy hears her at night, pleading with John. She wants him to listen to the men, to take care of their neighbors and not worry about those niggers in Buxton. John stands his ground. He follows all of the union's rules as the men go back to work.

Jimmy hears his parents fighting, hears the men in the town, worries about his dad, wonders if his dad is right. He is proud of his dad, but all those signs, *no niggers after dark*, those men in robes, he doesn't know what to believe.

One night during this time Jimmy is with his ma at a summer evening church service. While the minister is talking, the church doors slowly open and twenty robed men march down the aisle. They lay a bag of money on the preacher's podium and ask the good minister to join them in their righteous cause.

Ku Klux Klan   Source: Library of Congress

The men really frighten Jimmy. He asks his dad about it when he gets home. John sits him down and tries to explain the Klan to the frightened ten year old. *"Those men are cowards, Jimmy, hiding their faces, scaring women and children. Don't believe them. The union says everyone is equal. Believe the union."*

Jimmy asks his dad why the KKK never bother the people in Buxton. John tries to explain, *"I don't know, Jimmy. I think it's because the mine owner, Ben Buxton, has told everyone that if they treat the Negro miners badly they'll be fired. He'd probably run those cowards out of town."*

A few days after the KKK visit the church, Jimmy is hanging around the train station, hoping to catch a ride on the cart that picks up the occasional traveler. It is a cool autumn evening and only one person climbs down from the train, an elderly black man. It is almost dark and Jimmy is worried about what will happen if the man is in Hamilton after dark. The man gathers his bags, climbs on the wagon and tells the driver he wants to go to Buxton. Jimmy begs the driver to let him come along. He climbs up beside the man and they set off for Buxton. The man tells Jimmy that he is a preacher, a Methodist minister, and that he is going to Buxton to minister to the miners there. Jimmy tells him that his ma wants him to be a Methodist minister and that he just might do that. The minister starts singing some of the old hymns, softly. Jimmy joins in. As the sun goes down and the evening turns cold, the man notices that Jimmy is starting to shiver. He takes off his coat and wraps it around Jimmy's shoulders to keep him warm.

Jimmy remembers that man and that ride all of his life. He still talks about it when he is one hundred years old. Jimmy says that man and that ride help him decide just what he believes about "equality." He believes with John, with the union.

Unfortunately John's life as a coal miner affects his family in other, not so positive ways. Most of the miners are hard men. They work hard and when payday comes, many of them drink hard. So the children also have a dad who is a payday drunk. But still they love him. He is the one who reads them bible stories, takes his boys fishing, teaches them how to grow a big garden and to care for the chickens, pigs, and the occasional cow. He is kind to his daughters, encourages them, and is very proud when Faye becomes a teacher.

Christmas seems to be important to John. Somehow the children always have something in their stockings, an apple, an orange, a stick of peppermint candy. There is usually a tree decorated with strands of the popcorn they grow in their big garden. One year, work goes exceptionally well. There are no strikes. That is the year Jimmy and his brothers all get Bowie knives. The girls get rag dolls and books full of paper dolls. Ida does not want to spend the extra money on such foolishness. She wants the children to have new shoes and clothes. But maybe new clothes would not grace their lives in the way these simple gifts do, would not bring the same joy into their home in that little mining town.

That is the good John, the good dad. There is also the other John, the John of the payday drunks.

The children learn to steer their lives between these two dads, these two Johns. Sometimes they see other children come to school with obvious signs of the beatings they receive at home. When they see this they think, *At least Dad never hits us, never hurts us.* It's true, he never hurts them…physically.

JIMMY'S MOTHER, IDA PAULDING

Ida Paulding

Ida works so hard, there doesn't seem to be much energy or time left to dispense love to those six little bundles she cares for.

All of their clothes are washed on a wash board. It will be years before she has a simple wringer washing machine. John's work clothes are the hardest because of the coal dust. They always turn the water black. It takes many rinses to get them even close to clean.

Then there is the house. She sweeps, takes the rugs out, puts them over the clothesline and beats them with the rug beater. The windows are a constant challenge. Coal trucks rumble down the dusty streets, sending clouds of dirt everywhere. Ida's windows are always clean. In addition to the house, Ida has to keep the outhouses clean. She insists on two outhouses; one for the men, the other for the women and little children. Both outhouses are scrubbed clean every week.

Ida Paulding

Ida has a rain barrel on each side of the house. There is a pump right outside the back door but the water that comes out of the spout is brown with rust. She keeps a sock over the spout but the water that drains through the sock is still brown. So whenever Ida makes her beans she uses the water in the rain barrels. She also uses rain water to wash the family's hair and their church clothes.

There is a big wood cook stove in the kitchen. From long practice Ida knows just how much wood to use to get the temperature exactly right for baking her bread and pies. One side of the big stove has a deep reservoir that Ida always keeps full of water. When the cook stove is filled with brightly burning wood, the water Ida scoops out of the reservoir is hot, ready for dishes, baths and for scrubbing floors. The reservoir is the only source of hot water for the family.

Ida loves her children, lives for them and does her best to ensure that they will have a chance at a good life. But there are few hugs, stories or tender words. Maybe it's all just too much, too hard. Maybe all of her energy is taken up with the cooking, the cleaning, the washing and the hard, hard grind of her life.

But there are times of grace.

Left to Right: Coney, Ida, Tudie, Faye

If any of the children get sick, Ida nurses them, sometimes staying by their beds all night. Jimmy has frequent strep throats, runs high fevers and can't swallow anything but broth. There are no antibiotics in those days so Ida does what she can. If the sore throat lasts for more than a few days, Ida goes to the pasture, fills a sock with manure, wraps it in a towel, and places it around Jimmy's neck. The heat from the manure is supposed to draw out the infection. Jimmy usually gets better when she does this. Maybe he improves just to get away from the smell. He suffers the manure and does whatever she tells him to do to get better. He knows that when he opens his eyes in the near dark his ma will be there, will reach out, brush the hair off of his forehead, softly shush him.

So, if her tone is sometimes sharp when little feet track in dirt, or little hands reach for an extra piece of pie, the children do not seem to mind. She loves them. She is the one constant in their young lives.

JOHN AND IDA'S MARRIAGE

John grows up in Hootie, Illinois and Ida grows up in Virginia. No one really knows how or where they meet. In spite of the Paulding boys' reputation, Ida falls in love with this handsome young coal miner.

John is already working in the mines when they marry. He is a good worker, makes enough money to support his family, and is a loving father. He is also a payday drunk. Every payday John brings his money home and gives most of it to Ida. He keeps just enough money to get rip roaring drunk. This is the only time John drinks. He does not deprive his family.

When John comes stumbling in, middle of the night drunk, sometimes smelling of other women, Ida feels that she is coming unraveled. There are terrible fights, screaming, loud fights. The children pull the covers over their heads, try to lie quietly, to remain unnoticed while they wait for the storm to pass. Who is this man, this monster? Where is their dad, the dad who reads them stories, takes them fishing, and always makes sure they have something in their Christmas stockings? Where has he gone?

When their dad is really Dad, not a drunken monster, he seems to care for their mother. Even though the camp houses in Hamilton are new, they are still camp houses. Ida longs for a real home, a house with an upstairs and a big porch. Somehow John scrapes up enough money to buy a big white house just across the road from their original camp house. The upstairs has five bedrooms; one of them has a balcony, a perfect place to sleep on hot summer nights. The house comes with three huge lots. There is room for John's big gardens and the chickens and pigs.

Paulding Family Home

Things change for a while, get better. The payday binges become less violent in nature. There is a feeling of hope, but the drinking never stops.

Years slide by. The children all grow up and leave home. John and Ida are alone in the big white family home. John continues to walk down the train tracks and get drunk. One day Ida looks across the road and sees her daughter, Faye, in the yard of the camp house they all lived in when they first moved to Hamilton. Faye bought the house from the mining company and lives there alone. Ida walks across the road, sits down on the porch and decides to just stay there. She has finally had enough of the drunken nights, the violence and the smell of other women.

Original Camp House

Ida stays with Faye, and John continues to live in the big family home he bought for her. After Ida moves across the road, John continues to walk down the tracks to Lovilla and get drunk. But when he comes home, there is no one to argue with, no one but himself to be hurt by his stumbling drunkenness.

John Paulding

John and Ida start to build a relationship based on their new reality, their separate living arrangements. Every Sunday he walks across the road and has Sunday dinner with Ida and Faye. He calls Ida missus and thanks her for the meal. When the children come back to Hamilton to visit, they go to Faye and Ida's house. John always walks across the road to visit and have dinner with the family. When the children get ready to leave, John always tells them the same thing: *"I'll worry about you for the first half hour, then you're on your own."* Even though the children are all adults, they still enjoy their dad's unique way of telling them that he cares about them.

Ida, Faye, Nellie, Coney, John

John and Ida do not get a divorce. They never argue. They have found a way to live out their lives in peace, with mutual respect.

John and Ida

John dies when he is in his seventies and is buried in the Hamilton cemetery. Ida lives for a long time after John passes away. She stays in the camp house Faye bought so long ago. She loves to visit the cemetery and show her children and grandchildren where she will rest, right next to her husband John.

Entrance to Hamilton Cemetery

John and Ida's Grave: Hamilton Cemetery

JIMMY'S BROTHERS AND SISTERS

I like the old Chinese Proverb that says "You can never step in the same river twice." I really believe that. I also believe that no two children, even identical twins, ever have the same environment. Each child's experience is unique.

Dad had two brothers and three sisters. He was the youngest son. His baby sister Ethyl was born two years after him. Dad's stories certainly tell about his love for all of his siblings, but it seems to me that he was particularly close to his sisters Faye and Nellie. Nellie was the closest to him in age and they were best friends and playmates. Faye, the oldest child in the family, continued to love and care for him all of her life, just as she had when he was a little baby in Hootie, Illinois.

The history of my dad's brothers and sisters and what happened to them as they became adults, are all part of the stories my father told me.

JIMMY'S SISTER, FAYE

Faye

Faye is the oldest of the six children. Her first name is Lela, but everyone calls her Faye. When Jimmy is born she treats him like the little doll she never had. Faye carries him everywhere, dresses him in little smocks, wraps him in blankets and loves him.

She is smart and pretty and sometimes has a vagueness about her that is unexpected in a young child. Most of her friends quit school when they graduate from tenth grade. Faye continues, completes her normal training and receives her teaching certificate. She starts to teach when she is eighteen years old and never misses a year until she retires at sixty-eight.

When Faye starts teaching, she lives at home, walks miles to work in the little country schools around Hamilton, and gives most of her salary to her family,.

Faye (far right) and friends

A young man comes calling. He is a good young man, respectable. Faye seems to be in love. Her cheeks flush and her eyes shine whenever he comes to call on her. They take chaste walks, shy hands touching. Ida does not like this relationship. She forces Faye to end it, to tell the young man to never come to the house again.

No one really knows why Faye tells the young man goodbye, or why Ida is so opposed to the relationship. Maybe she really thinks it is the best thing for Faye. Perhaps she is afraid of losing the money Faye brings in for the family. Faye never talks about the young man, she just continues to teach and care for her family. She is still helping her family when Jimmy goes away to college. She helps to pay for her little brother's education. Faye's help is one of the main reasons Jimmy is able to go to college.

Faye saves her money and buys the little camp house the family lived in when they first came to Hamilton. It is right across the road from the big white house John bought for Ida. It is almost like she hasn't left home, but she has her own space and her own things.

Even though Faye is not married, she raises a daughter, her sister, Ethyl's, little girl. Ethyl returns to Hamilton one summer with her two children, Norman and Betty. Her marriage to Robert Townsend is over. While she is back in Hamilton, staying with her family, she gives birth to another child, a little girl she names Joann. When Joann is born, Faye keeps saying, *"Ethyl, I think you should give this baby to me. I'll take good care of her."*

Robert Townsend comes to Hamilton when Joann is almost three to claim his children. He takes Norman and Betty with him but he does not take Joann. He tells everyone that she is not his daughter. Shortly after that, Ethyl leaves Hamilton for good, leaving Joann in Hamilton to be raised by Faye, Ida, and John. Now Joann has two mamas, Mama Faye and Mama Ethyl. Faye takes Joann to visit Ethyl every summer and continues teaching and caring for her daughter.

Joann

When Faye is in her late fifties, she leaves Hamilton and moves to Deep River. She has a new job as a third grade teacher in Deep River, Iowa. Jimmy is the superintendent at Deep River. Faye and Joann move into Jimmy's home and live with them for a year. During her second year of teaching, Faye dates a local farmer and they make plans to get married. Faye is in her fifties and Joann is fifteen years old. When Faye marries Leamon Stevenson, she and Joann move out of Jimmy's house to start a new life.

Faye continues to teach at Deep River after her husband dies. When she retires, she returns to Hamilton. She remarries again when she is in her eighties. George McGilvrey is a nice man who cares for her in her old age. When Faye passes away, she is buried in the Hamilton cemetery. Faye is back home again, not far from the camp house, the family home and the little white Methodist church. She is buried near her ma and her dad. Hopefully at peace.

Faye's Grave

JIMMY'S BROTHER, CONEY

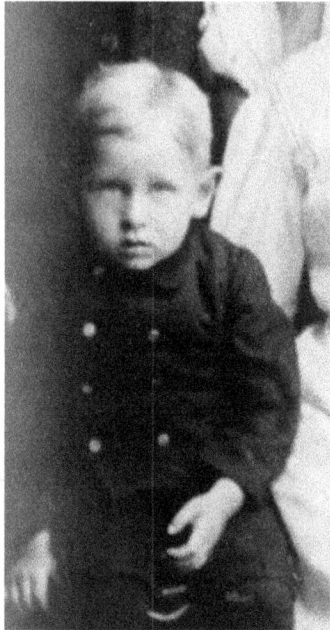

Coney

Coney is six years older than Jimmy, the oldest boy in the family. He has those blue, blue Paulding eyes, big Paulding ears and a teenage addiction to religion. Hamilton is a coal mining town, a place where men work hard, drink hard, and spend a lot more time in the pool hall than in the pristine little white Methodist church.

On summer evenings, Jimmy watches as Coney stands outside the pool hall, reading scripture, singing hymns and trying to save souls, souls who have absolutely no interest in salvation. Sometimes other boys join Coney to sing and pray with him. The men come and go, most of them ignore the boys. A few spit tobacco juice at their feet, some nod pleasantly. None are saved. Coney continues to pray for the sinners inside.

Jimmy does not join his brother. He doesn't know whether to be proud or embarrassed. He knows that more than likely his Uncle Shorty is one of the men in the pool hall, one of the men who will go home drunk tonight, one of the men who has no interest in scriptures and hymns.

Usually Jimmy watches for a while, then shrugs his shoulders and runs down the dusty street to join his friends at the depot. They walk around town, spotting butts and smoking.

Coney falls in love with his cousin, Bernice. Bernice is also very religious. She has a beautiful singing voice and loves music. Their families object to their love but they get married anyway and move to Des Moines. There seems to be some concern about Bernice's health, but none of that matters to Coney. He is happy in his marriage, is a good husband, provider and father.

Coney and Bernice

Coney gets a job driving a delivery truck for Wonder Bread and works for them until he retires. They buy a house on the east side and have three children: Richard, Dorothy and Kenneth. Dorothy and Kenneth both have musical talent and are wonderful singers. Kenneth can play the piano by ear. When he hears a song he can just sit down and play it. It seems that Bernice brings many gifts to the Paulding family.

When Coney brings his family back to Hamilton on Sundays, he always brings Ida plenty of bread and rolls. When they visit, Coney loves to sit in the little parlor and call out to the kitchen. He always says the same thing: *"Is dinner ready yet, Ma?"* Ma usually doesn't answer. She is too busy working, getting the big Sunday dinner ready.

Coney, Bernice, and Ida

JIMMY'S BROTHER, TUDIE

Tudie

Jimmy's brother, Tudie, is four years his senior. Tudie's real name is Ray Paulding, but no one ever calls him Ray. He is always Tudie.

Tudie is beyond shy. From the beginning, he melts away whenever too many people are around. School is torture with its closed doors, too many children, too much noise and always the teachers. They keep trying to get him to understand, to do his school work. Tudie can read but when he is called on to read in front of the class, he freezes, unable to utter a single word. Tudie can do his sums just fine in his seat. When he is called on to do the work at the blackboard, none of the numbers make sense.

Some of the teachers understand and let him do his work in his own way. Most of them do not. As soon as he finishes eighth grade, Tudie quits walking through the school room door.

Church is another too confining place. There are too many people, too much noise and the preacher hurts his head with his booming voice. He goes, pulling against Ida's hand. *"Don't make me go, Ma. Don't make me, please, Ma."*

Of course his ma makes him go. When he gets too big to drag through the church door, Tudie's time in church is over.

When kids pick on Tudie and call him stupid, he never defends himself. He usually runs away or curls up in a ball and silently suffers their taunts and blows. He is not stupid. He is simply a shy, gentle boy who will grow up to be a shy, gentle man.

Tudie is happiest when he is in the woods or hanging out at Cedar Creek. When he is very young, he starts stealing away to Tennessee Hollow, the big woods that are about a mile from his home. The summer his grandpa Jacob brings him an Indian suit, he wears it constantly. Ida has a hard time getting it off of him so she can wash it. When he walks through the big woods with his bow, he feels like a real Indian, imagining tipis, wood smoke.

Tudie

Tudie learns how to find the shy morels and the sweet black raspberries. Thanks to Tudie, Ida always has plenty of berries for her pies. In the fall he gathers hickory nuts and walnuts and spends hours cracking them, picking out the nuts.

Sometimes Ida tells Tudie to go to Snack's store to get a few groceries. When this happens he goes to find Jimmy and talks him into going to the store for him. Tudie is too shy to go, unable to force himself to go in the store and tell the person working there what his mother wants.

Two things happen in Tudie's young life that some family members use to explain his shyness. When he is about ten, he and his friend, Johnny Lickliter, fall into an old abandoned well. Neither boy is hurt, but Tudie is terrified about being trapped in that closed, dark place. Then when he is sixteen, and tries to go down in the mines to work with John, they hit a bad air pocket and Tudie is gassed. They have to carry him out of the mine. He is unconscious and when he eventually comes around he seems dazed and confused. He never goes back in the mines. Whenever Jimmy talks about Tudie's shyness he says, *"Some people say Tudie changed after he was gassed in the mine, but Tudie was always like that."*

When World War Two starts, Tudie is ordered to report for duty. He leaves home as he is ordered, but that night he sneaks away and walks back home. The next day, Ida goes to see the family doctor. The doctor writes a letter to the draft board and the army doesn't bother Tudie again.

Tudie builds himself a little house out behind Faye's Hamilton home and lives there until he dies.

Tudie and Faye

Tudie's Shack

He remains shy, works for local farmers, cuts wood and gathers coal off the railroad tracks. He builds things and paints them all red, white and blue. His yard is full of "sculptures." One side of his house is covered with the names of all of the presidents of the United States. He collects wagon wheels, coins, old marbles, and comic books. And as he has done all his life, Tudie continues to spend a lot of time in the woods. When Ida dies, he gives his morels and raspberries to other housewives. He keeps the nuts for himself, for winter.

Tudie in Hamilton

Tudie lives until he is eighty-six and is buried in the Hamilton cemetery. The inscription on his tombstone reads: *"One with nature."*

Tudie's Grave

JIMMY'S SISTER, NELL

Nellie

Little Nellie, who poked Jimmy in the belly when he was born, is never afraid to poke any of her brothers or sisters. She is a tiny girl, tiny and fearless. Jimmy always tells his friends, *"Nobody messes with Nell."*

In the days before girls wore pants, Nell is as much of a tomboy as her skirts will allow. Nellie is tough but there is also something wonderfully, indefinably good about Nell. People feel happy when they are around her, sense her goodness and feel she is a blessing. Nellie, a big blessing in a tiny body.

Nellie

When Jimmy is ten, he signs up for a paper route, dreaming of grand prizes and money. After three mornings of getting up before dawn and trudging through town carrying a heavy bag of papers, he decides he doesn't really need those prizes or money. Nell says she will take over the route and she does. Every morning, no matter what the weather, she climbs out of bed and delivers the papers. Her customers love her and often invite her in for hot chocolate on cold winter mornings. Nellie keeps the paper route until she graduates from high school and moves to Des Moines.

Nellie (in front) and friends

When Nellie gets to Des Moines, she lives with her Uncle Lou and Aunt Judy and their three daughters. She finds a job working in a garment factory. She works hard and gives part of her salary to her Uncle Lou. Every chance she gets, she goes home to Hamilton to see her ma and her dad.

Nellie (left) & her cousin, Irma

She also has a lot of fun, goes out, buys some daring flapper clothes and falls in love with a handsome young man, Eddie Murray.

Nellie (left) and friend

Nellie and Eddie get married and move in with his parents. Nellie continues to work, gets pregnant, and has a little baby girl, Phyllis. Things do not go well with the marriage. Nellie wants them to move out of his parent's house and get their own place. Eddie wants to stay with his parents. Eddie and his family are Catholic. Nellie feels shut out of that part of their life and does not want to convert.

Nellie moves out and leaves her daughter, Phyllis, in the care of Eddie's sister, Pearly. When Nellie moves out, she gets a job working in the housewares department at the downtown Montgomery Ward Store. She works there until she retires in her late sixties.

Nellie continues to go home to Hamilton almost every weekend. Sometimes she brings Phyllis with her. Phyllis is a beautiful little girl who will grow into a beautiful woman. Nellie seems content to leave her daughter with Pearly and see her on the occasional weekend.

Phyllis and her cousin Dickey Buchanan in Hamilton

In the 1940's, Nellie marries Harry Baker. They have many happy years, buy a house on Cleveland Street and save up for a new car and a boat.

Harry and Nellie

The first day they take their new boat out on the Des Moines River it is a bright, sunny day, a day made for happiness, not tragedy. But as they pass close to the riverbank, a huge tree falls down and crashes into the boat. Nellie and Harry's lives are changed forever.

Nellie has a broken arm, broken ribs and a sprained neck. Harry, who tried to protect Nellie from the tree, is not so lucky. His spinal cord is severed and he is paralyzed from his waist down. He will never walk again.

When Harry is released from the hospital, Nellie takes him home. Harry's mother moves in with them and Nellie returns to work. Harry lives for many years and Nellie and her mother-in-law continue to care for him. When her mother-in-law dies, Nellie quits work so she can continue to care for Harry.

Harry and Nellie

After Harry passes away, Nellie continues to care for people. When her ma gets sick, she brings her to Des Moines for the winter. When her brother, Coney, loses his eyesight, she takes him in and cares for him until he regains enough sight to be on his own again. When her nieces and nephews need help or a hug, she is always there, never turning anyone away.

Years pass and when Nellie is in her seventies she decides to have an adventure. She and her cousin, Irma, buy Greyhound Bus Passes. They travel all over the United States, going west to Oregon, south to New Orleans, then to New York and Chicago. One day, when they are in a hotel in Chicago, they leave their room door open and a man sneaks in and grabs Nellie's purse off the bed. She sees him from the bathroom, runs out yelling and starts chasing him down the hall. Even though Nellie is seventy-five, she is still fast, but luckily not that fast. She doesn't catch him. When she tells the hotel manager about it, the manager just shakes his head in amazement and asks her what in the world she would have done if she had caught him.

Nellie continues to live in her home on Cleveland Street until she dies at the blessed age of one hundred. She never quits smoking her beloved cigs, never quits helping people and she never loses that wonderful, indefinable quality that makes you feel blessed to be with her. Nellie does not choose to go "home" to be buried. She is buried in Des Moines, next to her husband, Harry.

JIMMY'S SISTER, ETHYL

Ethyl

Ethyl is the youngest of the six Paulding children. She is just a baby when they move to Hamilton. Ethyl seems to be a happy little girl. She becomes fast friends with her cousin, Wilma, Uncle Shorty's daughter. She goes to school and church. As she gets older, she displays a *"wild streak,"* which really worries Ida.

Ida tries to settle her down and steer her in a more modest direction. However, Ida is not able to control her youngest daughter as easily as she controlled Faye. Before Ethyl graduates from high school, she and her cousin, Wilma, leave home and go to Chicago. They both find jobs and enjoy city life.

Ethyl meets a young man, Robert Townsend, falls in love and gets married. He seems to be a nice young man. They have two children, Norman and Betty, but after five years, things begin to fall apart. Robert accuses Ethyl of being unfaithful.

Ethyl returns to Hamilton and lives with her ma and her sister Faye. While she is in Hamilton, she gives birth to a baby girl, Joann. Faye feels a special connection to this baby as soon as Joann is born.

When Joann is three, Robert Townsend comes to Hamilton. He loads Norman and Betty in his car and leaves. He tells Ethyl and Ida that Joann is not his child and he drives away. Joann watches as her brother and sister are being taken away. Rumors swirl around the little coal mining town, around the family.

Shortly after Robert Townsend takes Norman and Betty away, Ethyl leaves Hamilton for good.

She returns to Chicago, leaving Joann behind to be raised by Faye and Ida. Faye now has custody of the little baby she always wanted for her own. Three year old Joann has just lost her brother and sister, and been abandoned by her mother.

After she returns to Chicago, Ethyl marries Eddie Fick. Eddie works in the auto industry in Belvedere, Illinois. Ethyl and Eddie have six children, but the marriage is not a happy one. The beautiful, laughing girl becomes a worn, sad shadow of herself.

Ethyl rarely returns home to Hamilton. Nellie and Faye take Joann to see her Mama Ethyl every summer. When they come home to Iowa they worry about Ethyl; about her marriage and how sad she seems.

Ethyl, the youngest of the six children, is the first to die. The last years of her life, the years in Belvedere with Eddie, are very hard. Hopefully she hung on to some happier memories of her childhood in Hamilton.

Jimmy and Ethyl

JIMMY'S EXTENDED FAMILY: THE MCCLURES

JIMMY'S GRANDMA AND GRANDPA McCLURE

Jimmy's grandma and grandpa McClure are married in 1860. Grandma McClure had been married once before to Steven Rhea. They had one son. After Steven dies, she marries Abraham, and they have four daughters and one son.

Jimmy's grandfather McClure dies in 1919 when Jimmy is ten. He doesn't have many memories of his grandpa, but Grandma McClure and his aunt Suze are a big part of his childhood.

Every summer, Grandma McClure (who everyone calls Biddy) and Aunt Suze come to Hamilton to visit Ida's family.

Left to right: Suze, Grandma Biddy, Faye, Bernice (holding Richard),
Coney, John, Ethyl, Ida, Nellie

Matilda Jane Price (Biddy) McClure

Ida (far left), Biddy (front), Suze (far right) and unknown relatives

Sometimes Biddy stays for months at a time. The children love Biddy and enjoy having her in their home. She helps Ida bake pies and is not as cranky as their ma when they want an extra piece. She holds the little ones, rocks them, and tells them stories about her childhood.

Biddy and grandchild

Sometimes when Biddy is sleeping and John comes home drunk, she starts to moan. Her OOOOOO, OOOOOOO, OOOOOOO reverberates through the whole house. The children get scared and wonder if their tiny grandma has died and turned into a terrifying ghost.

No matter how drunk John is, when Biddy starts to moan and wail, he always tries to reassure her, telling her over and over: *"Now, now, Biddy. You know I would never hurt you."*

These visits from her ma and Suze are important to Ida, a time for her to reconnect with her family. They make the time between Ida's visits home to Virginia seem less lonely.

Ida in Virginia

Ida's mother, Biddy, has an amazing life. Biddy lives through the civil war and faces many other challenges. When she is a little girl, she survives an Indian raid by hiding in her family's barn. Some members of her family are killed, but Biddy stays safely hidden and lives to be one hundred years old (see her obituary in the archives for the full story).

Although she is a small woman, a "biddy," her strength and loving ways help to shape many generations.

Ida, Biddy, & Suze

McClure Grave

JIMMY'S EXTENDED FAMILY: THE PAULDINGS

JIMMY'S GRANDMA AND GRANDPA PAULDING

Jacob Paulding and Nancy Wineland Paulding

Jacob and Nancy have ten children, five of whom die in infancy. Five children live into adulthood: Louis, Susan, Emma, John, and Audry.

Jacob Paulding is a Civil War veteran and a lifelong coal miner. After the Civil War, he moves from Indiana to St. David, Illinois to work in the mines. He lives in St. David until he dies at ninety-four, one of the oldest Civil War veterans in the county.

Jacob Paulding

When Jimmy is three years old, his grandma and grandpa Paulding come to Hamilton for a visit. They take the train from St David, Illinois. It is a long train ride but Jimmy's Grandpa Jacob is determined to stay in touch with his sons. Grandpa Jacob Paulding is a tall, handsome, white haired man. Sometimes he holds Jimmy on his lap and sings to him.

Jimmy's Grandma Paulding scurries around silently. She is a small, round woman with grey hair that is pulled back in a proper bun. She glares at unexpected noises and jumps when little hands reach for her and touch her skirts.

Grandpa Jacob brings all of the children gifts. Jimmy gets a buckskin suit and a toy gun. Tudie, Jimmy's older brother, receives an Indian outfit and a bow and arrow, a gift he cherishes. John wonders: *how in the world did my dad know exactly what would suit my quiet, solitary little boy? How did he know that a bow and arrows would be perfect for Tudie?*

Left to Right: Jimmy, Faye, Nellie, Ida holding Ethyl,
Tudie and Coney wearing new clothes – a gift from Jacob

Jimmy's grandparents stay for a month. When they leave, the children miss their tall, kind grandpa. They do not think much about their grandma and do not really miss her.

His grandma and grandpa Paulding come back several times and stay with Jimmy's family. On one visit, everyone is at Jimmy's house for Sunday dinner. Jimmy's Aunt Ruth and Uncle Shorty are there with their little girl, Wilma. They are all gathered around the big, long kitchen table. Grandpa Jacob is talking and laughing with Aunt Ruth, telling some of his outrageous tall tales. Everyone is laughing, the little ones giggling and feeling happy. Jimmy's grandma gets up, leaves the table and stalks out the back door. Shorty looks over at John. *"What in the hell is bothering her now?"*

John shrugs his shoulders. He doesn't have any idea what has set his mother off. When Jimmy's Aunt Ruth comes out of the kitchen door, Grandma Paulding is waiting. She throws lye at Aunt Ruth's face. Luckily Aunt Ruth turns her face back toward Shorty just as the lye flies at her. The lye hits the back of her head and the left side of her face.

Everyone starts screaming. Jimmy's mom quickly takes Ruth to the kitchen and holds her head over the dishpan, rinsing and rinsing and rinsing, trying to get the lye off of her face and out of her hair.

Grandma Paulding rocks back and forth, back and forth. *"My husband, my Jacob. You, you smile and smile…my Jacob."* Grandpa Jacob leads her away.

Uncle Shorty paces outside the door, swearing and sweating. The children sit quietly, a frozen tableau. Little Wilma cries for her mama. Uncle Shorty picks her up and continues to pace.

Grandpa Jacob takes his wife home on the next train. She does not come again. When Grandpa Jacob comes back to visit, he comes alone.

Coney (holding Dorothy), John and Jacob in Hamilton – Four Generations of Pauldings

Paulding Cemetery Plot St. David, IL: Jacob and Nancy's grave and three infants

JIMMY'S UNCLE LOU

Uncle Lou is the oldest of the Paulding boys. When he arrives in Hamilton he meets Judy Simms and they soon marry. They buy a small house in Des Moines and have three daughters: Irma, Irene and Vera. Although they live in Des Moines, a lifelong bond is forms between Nellie and Lou's daughters.

Uncle Lou is a lover of music and is an excellent violinist. He teaches all of his daughters to play an instrument. They are very talented and often compete at the state fair.

Uncle Lou is the only Paulding brother who doesn't seem to have a problem with liquor and domestic violence. He is mostly a peaceful man, a man of music, a good husband and father. There is another thing that sets Lou apart from his brothers. Lou is an atheist, does not believe in the existence of God. While it's true that John and Shorty never go to church, they still believe, still read their children bible stories.

Jimmy sometimes worries about Uncle Lou, about the fact that he doesn't believe in God. One day when Lou and Jimmy are fishing, the sun is hot and Lou is lounging under a tree enjoying the shade. Jimmy is down by the creek, checking his lines when Uncle Lou calls out to him.

"Jimmy, get up here in the shade. What do you think God made this tree for?"

After that, Jimmy thinks that maybe Uncle Lou isn't such an atheist after all.

Sometimes when Uncle Lou comes to Hamilton, he and Jimmy catch a freight train and ride it back to Des Moines. The engineer usually slows the train down for Uncle Lou. Jimmy stays with them for a few days. Lou tells Jimmy that he enjoys having another "man" in the house.

When he and Lou take a walk in the evening, Lou sometimes has a beer and smokes a cigarette. Whenever that happens he always tells Jimmy, *"We don't have to mention this to Aunt Judy."*

Uncle Lou, Aunt Judy and the girls are not as big a part of Jimmy's life as his Hamilton relatives. But in that family he has a glimpse of a home where fathers do not come home drunk on payday, where there are no violent fights, where children do not shiver under their covers, waiting for the storm to pass.

It is good that he has the opportunity to see this different kind of life, this different family. It is good that he knows that men don't have to drink or fight to be men.

JIMMY'S UNCLE SHORTY

Jimmy's Uncle Shorty's real name is Audry Paulding. He is handsome, full of shit and the youngest and wildest of the Paulding brothers.

Shorty always walks on the edge. He steals his first chickens when he's a teenager, still living in Illinois. He and his future brother-in-law, Humpy Baxter, are driving around the dusty dirt roads, enjoying a warm sunny day when they come across a large flock of chickens who are also out enjoying the sun. Humpy stops the car, the boys get out and start catching the chickens. They stuff them in a wire cage that is tied on the back of their car. The farmer hears the commotion and runs out, asking them what they are doing. Shorty very calmly tells him that their crate fell off of the car and their chickens got loose. The farmer helps the boys catch the chickens and waves them on their way.

Humpy Baxter

When Shorty moves to Hamilton he falls in love with Ruth Simms, Aunt Judy's sister. John tells Shorty, *"I don't know how you and Lou got the two prettiest girls in the county."*

Uncle Shorty and Aunt Ruth move into a camp house just down the street from John and Ida. They have two daughters: Wilma and Baby. Wilma and Jimmy's sister, Ethyl, are about the same age and become inseparable.

Shorty continues to steal chickens all of his life. No one is quite sure why he does it. He doesn't need to steal chickens to keep his family from starving. He is a mule driver in the mines and is highly prized for his ability to move the coal from the depths of the mine to the surface. Sometimes when he steals chickens, he gets caught and they put him in jail. No matter what Shorty does, the mine owners come to the jail and get their mule driver out, get him back on the job.

Shorty is a mule driver, a chicken thief, a hard drinker and a violent, brawling man. When Shorty comes home drunk, there isn't just yelling and fighting. He sometimes takes one of his guns out in the back yard, throws things up in the air and shoots at them. People can hear the gunshots all over town.

One day Shorty goes on a rampage at the pool hall. The pool hall in Hamilton is a favorite hangout for the miners and the older teenage boys. In the front of the pool hall, there is a long bar and four big windows that look out over the dusty town streets. There are three pool tables in the back.

One summer, the manager of the pool hall decides to run a punch card game. If you get all of your numbers punched, you win a watch. Shorty gets all of his numbers punched and goes up to the bar to collect his watch. Unfortunately, the manager has already given the watch to another fellow, a man who filled his punch card earlier in the day. Shorty starts throwing pool balls at the long mirror behind the bar and through the big front windows. Glass flies everywhere.

After all of the windows are broken, Shorty storms out and goes home to get his gun. Johnny Foster, the current sheriff, gathers a small posse and they head down the street toward Shorty's house. Jimmy watches as they chase Shorty down the street and out of town. They eventually catch him and put him in jail. It costs the mine owners a lot to get their mule driver out of jail this time.

Jimmy is only eight when Shorty wrecks the pool hall. He is terrified when he hears the noise and the gunshots. He doesn't know if his uncle is alive or dead, doesn't know if his uncle has killed someone.

Two days after Shorty gets out of jail, he sneaks up behind the pool hall and starts a fire. As the flames start to lick at the back wall of the pool hall, Shorty runs down the road to his house. Luckily John happens to step outside for a minute, sees the flames, runs to the pool hall and is able to get the fire out. He knows his younger brother has set the fire, but says nothing to anyone.

That same summer, Uncle Shorty brings violence to Jimmy's home. Early one summer morning Jimmy hears someone banging on the front door. He goes downstairs and sees two of Aunt Ruth's brothers with their guns strapped on, demanding that John Paulding turn Shorty over. It seems that they were all in a big poker game the night before and Shorty made off with all of the

Simms boys' money. John tells the men that he hasn't seen Shorty and he certainly wouldn't be hiding him. *"Get those guns out of here, there are young children in the house,"* John says. The Simms boys leave. They find Shorty later that day and beat him up, but they never find their money.

Uncle Shorty. Mule driver, chicken thief, bringer of violence.

He is also Jimmy's uncle, an uncle who takes him hunting, fishing and, on one memorable day, takes him down into the mines. When Jimmy finds out that Uncle Shorty is going to take him down in the mines, he can hardly wait…he feels very proud to be riding with Shorty behind the mules.

Mules in the Coal Mines   Source: Library Of Congress

When they are about halfway down, Shorty tells the mules to *"whoa." "Want to show you something, Jimmy."* Jimmy feels a little scared. He's not sure what is going to happen. Then Shorty reaches out and turns the lanterns off. It is a dark like no dark Jimmy has ever experienced. Before he can even catch his breath, he hears Shorty tell the mules to *"Getup"* and the mules set off down the tracks in the pitch black darkness.

Jimmy cries out, grabs Shorty. *"Stop, Shorty. Stop. The mules can't see."*

Shorty laughs and laughs. *"Jimmy, didn't you know, these mules are both blind. They've worked so long in the dark they can't see a thing."* And with that, Shorty and Jimmy continue going down in the mine in total darkness, trusting the blind mules to find their way.

Uncle Shorty. Sometimes kind. Sometimes frightening. Part of the family, part of Jimmy's life.

Another important person in Jimmy's life is his Aunt Ruth, Shorty's wife. Everyone is terrified of Shorty, but everybody loves his wife, Aunt Ruth. She is the essence of kindness, a gentle, religious woman, a good mother.

Aunt Ruth loves her first daughter, Wilma, but her second daughter, Baby, is the child of her heart. Baby is probably the prettiest little girl in Hamilton. She has curly, golden hair, blue eyes, and is a happy, laughing little girl who seems to brighten everyone's life. Baby is everyone's pet.

One day, four year old Baby gets sick and doesn't get better. The doctor is called but is not able to do anything. A few days later, Baby dies and a part of Aunt Ruth seems to die with her. She is inconsolable, cries all day long and stops taking care of Wilma and the house. She stops eating and doesn't cook meals for her family. She refuses to go to church and will not talk to the preacher when he tries to comfort her. Every day she wanders down the road crying, heading for the cemetery. When she gets there, she lays across Baby's grave, sobbing uncontrollably, digging her fists into the dirt.

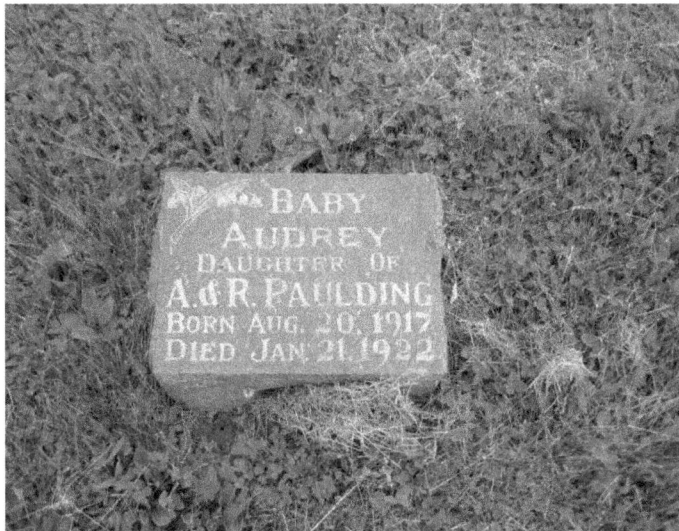

Baby's Grave in the Hamilton Cemetery

Sometimes Shorty has to go to the cemetery to pull her off of the grave. Sometimes it is Ida who tries to get her to come home, to leave the cemetery.

During this time Ruth's daughter, Wilma, spends most of her days at Ida's house, playing with her cousin, Ethyl. She eats her meals with Ida and John's family.

Months pass and Ruth slowly tries to put her life back together. She starts caring for Wilma again, cleans the house, cooks and goes back to church.

Her daughter, Wilma, leaves home before she finishes school. She and her cousin, Ethyl, go to Chicago, Wilma marries Richard Buchanan and they have a little boy, Dickey. Ruth helps Wilma take care of Dickey and he brings new happiness to Ruth's life. Dickey grows up to be a fine young man. Ruth is very proud of him.

Dickey Buchanan and Phyllis

When Dickey is three, Ruth takes him to the Fourth of July celebration in Bussey. After he sees the parade, Dickey tells Ruth he wants to ride his tricycle in the parade. So the next year Ruth decorates Dickey's trike. Then she decides to decorate her own three wheeled bicycle so they can both ride in the parade. From then on, Ruth rides her bicycle in every Fourth of July parade until she passes away. If you go to Hamilton today and ask people about Ruth Paulding, they will probably smile and tell you about how she always rode her bicycle in the parade.

Ruth's Bicycle

Shorty and Ruth's Grave

JIMMY PAULDING

Jimmy Paulding

Jimmy loves living in Hamilton. All of his days are full, but summer days are the best. The mines are frequently closed in the summer. If there are no pay checks, there are no payday benders. Things are more peaceful at home.

As Jimmy grows, so does his freedom. At first he stays close to home, his world defined by the post office on one end of his street and the pool hall and grocery store on the other end. Soon the whole town is his playground. He and his friends run together in the summer evenings, playing tag, ball and smoking illicit cigarettes.

Every year, Jimmy begs his dad to take him along when he and Coney go fishing at Cedar Creek. It seems to Jimmy that he would give anything to be able to go along, to have that time with his dad and big brother.

One evening when Jimmy is eight, sitting in church, listening to the preacher, his brother, Coney, slips into the pew beside him and whispers *"Dad says you're old enough to come with us now."*

Jimmy can hardly believe it, he is really going on an adventure with his dad. Ida tries to catch his eye, to make him sit back down, but Jimmy is already out the door. He follows his dad down through the cemetery, to the path that leads to Cedar Creek. He walks proudly beside Coney, head high, shoulders back.

After they put out their trot lines, John makes a fire and fries up some potatoes and onions. He tells Jimmy that if they are lucky, they will have fresh fish for breakfast. They are almost always lucky when they go fishing at Cedar Creek. Jimmy never misses another overnight fishing trip.

Sometimes they sleep on the bank, under the stars. Sometimes they sleep in the ice house that sits on one of the banks of the creek.

In the winter, men go to the creek and cut out big chunks of ice. They pack it in sawdust and put it in the ice house. All summer long, they deliver ice to the houses in town. When the ice is all gone, the icehouse makes a perfect place to spend the night, the sweet smelling sawdust a perfect bed.

Sometimes their dad takes Jimmy and Coney all the way to the Des Moines River to fish. It is always an exciting trip. They hitch their horse, Lady, to the cart and take off.

John and Jimmy with Lady

The Des Moines river is much bigger than Cedar Creek, so big it's almost scary. Sometimes these trips last for days. Jimmy cherishes this time with his dad and brother and develops a lifelong love of fishing.

All of Jimmy's friends learn how to swim at an early age. Sometimes they swim in the big quarry at the edge of town. Mostly they go to Cedar Creek. The boys build dams in the creek, trying to make their swimming hole deeper. They tie logs together, make crude rafts and float down the creek until their "pirate ship" runs aground. Some of Jimmy's happiest days are spent at Cedar Creek.

One day Jimmy and Tudie are down at Cedar Creek swimming when Tudie yells, *"here come the girls, Jimmy, here come the girls."* Jimmy climbs out of the water, grabs his britches and tries to jump over a barbwire fence. He cuts his left arm, and blood spurts everywhere. Even though he is only twelve years old years old, Jimmy knows he is in serious trouble. He and Tudie run to Mrs. Liebie's house. She gets the bleeding stopped, bandages his arm and sends him home. Jimmy always remembers Mrs. Liebie. He still has the scar from the barbwire cut when he is a very old man.

Summer is special for so many reasons. Jimmy learns to garden and works hard with his dad. He loves growing the food that Ida will use to feed the family. Gardening is another lifelong passion, another skill he learns from his dad.

John also keeps a few chickens, pigs and sometimes a cow or goat for milk. So even when the mines are closed for part of the summer, the family always has enough to eat.

In the summer, the other miners come and sit with John. They usually bring along a bottle. John always refuses to drink. He tells his friends that if he can't afford to buy the stuff, he can't afford to drink it.

Yes, summer is good. Summer is a golden time, a time Jimmy holds tight in his memories.

Ethyl and Jimmy with their dogs

Music is another golden part of Jimmy's young life. From the time he is little, Jimmy loves music and sings all of the hymns in church. When he is ten, Ida decides to send him to Faye Snack (who owns the local grocery store) for piano lessons. Faye loves music, loves teaching piano to the miners' children.

Faye Snack

The lessons cost a dime a week. No one knows where Ida gets that dime, but she always seems to manage to get the things her youngest son needs.

Jimmy walks down the block every week, knocks on Faye Snack's door, takes off his cap and sits down at the piano. She tries to teach Jimmy good manners along with his music.

Ida thinks he needs a piano at home so he can practice. John scrapes up enough money to buy an old player piano. Jimmy practices every day. He is soon good enough to play for the church services. Ida sits proudly in the pews, listening to her youngest son.

Jimmy's early childhood is a full and happy one, but the world really opens up for him when he starts school. From the time he can walk, Jimmy begs his ma to let him go to school with his brothers and sisters. Of course, Jimmy has to wait until he is five to start first grade.

The first day of school he walks proudly down the road holding his sister, Nellie's, hand. His clothes are mended hand-me-downs, squeaky clean with much washing. Ida finds a little cap for him to wear and he sets it jauntily on his head and starts out on another adventure.

Jimmy Paulding at School

Unlike his brother, Tudie, Jimmy thrives in school. He is a sociable kid, and loves to be around the children and teachers. The big white school house becomes one of his favorite places. He especially likes English and history.

Jimmy Paulding at school: front row, sixth from the right

Jimmy is disappointed when he finds out the school in Hamilton only goes through tenth grade.

Jimmy Paulding 6th Grade

Many of the young people who complete tenth grade stop their education and go to work and get married. Ida encourages Jimmy to get his high school diploma. She does not want to lose this son to the mines. She believes he has the ability to do many things, dreams of having a minister in the family.

Jimmy enrolls in high school in nearby Bussey. Sometimes he and the other kids from Hamilton walk the two miles to Bussey. Sometimes they hop one of the freight trains that rumble between the towns and arrive at school windblown and triumphant.

The school is much larger than the little Hamilton school, but Jimmy quickly adjusts. He makes the baseball team and is a pretty good hitter. One day he hits a double and starts tearing around the bases. Halfway to second, the safety pin that is holding his overalls up breaks and his britches fall down. Everyone starts laughing. Jimmy just pulls his britches up and makes it safely to second base.

He tries out for a school play and, much to his amazement, gets a part playing opposite Geraldine Brady. He has had a crush on Geraldine ever since she walked into the Hamilton school four years ago. During the play he even gets to give her a chaste kiss on the cheek. He doesn't think life can get any better that this. He loves high school.

Jimmy in high school

Jimmy Paulding's High School Graduation Picture

When Jimmy graduates from high school, he goes down in the mines and works with his dad.

Coal Mine near Hamilton

Being in the mines with his dad increases Jimmy's respect for John and for the work he does to support his family.

Ida fights this move, insisting that Jimmy can have a different life. She wants him to go to college. College sounds like a dream, something that has nothing to do with a boy from Hamilton, with a boy from the coal mines of southern Iowa.

This is another struggle that Ida wins. Jimmy enrolls in John Fletcher College, a bible school located in Oskaloosa, Iowa. In four years he will be an ordained Methodist minister, and Ida's dreams for her youngest son will be fulfilled.

Ida hitchhikes to Albia, goes to the clothing store and charges clothes for her son, the son who will be a preacher.

Paying for Jimmy's education is a big challenge for his family. Faye helps, using part of her teacher's salary to pay for her little brother's tuition. Jimmy takes any odd job he can find and waits tables in the college dining hall to help pay for his room and board. John, the master gardener, brings a truckload of fresh vegetables to the college to help meet expenses.

Jimmy immerses himself in college life.

Jimmy playing football at college

He really loves English class and develops a lifelong love of Shakespeare. To be ordained, Jimmy naturally has to take many religion classes. As his college years pass, and he is introduced to the world's great religions, he finds there is more to the world than Christianity. He starts to question things, including some of his basic beliefs. Things that seemed so straightforward when he was a boy in Hamilton, sitting next to Ida, listening to the preacher, no longer seem so simple or true. When Jimmy begins to question his faith during his college years, the simple days of believing that every word of the Bible is true are over forever. From that point on, his faith becomes a much more complicated, personal thing.

The summers of his college years are spent far away from Hamilton. One year he travels to North Dakota to work in the wheat harvest. He buys a Harley Davidson motorcycle and rides all over the state, going from one job to the next.

Another summer he goes to Chicago and lives with his cousin Roscoe and works in the Sands Hotel. Jimmy runs the elevator and flirts with all of the beautiful, sophisticated women. Jimmy loves being out on his own and making money to help pay for his tuition. But he is often homesick and is always happy to get back to Hamilton.

John Fletcher College is a bible school and has very strict rules for its students. Drinking and smoking are both punishable with expulsion. In his senior year, Jimmy and some of his friends start sneaking into town to smoke forbidden cigarettes. Jimmy stays clear of the liquor but his best friend is caught drinking three weeks before graduation and is sent home with nothing to show for his four years of effort.

Jimmy completes his work, graduates with good grades and, most importantly, graduates as an ordained Methodist minister. Jimmy is the first person in his family to graduate from college. Ida feels such a sense of pride and relief. She has sacrificed so much for this, fought so many battles on behalf of her youngest son. Now it has all come true. This son will have a different life. He will be a respected man of God.

Jim Paulding's College Graduation Picture

Jimmy is assigned to a small church in Marne, Iowa. Jimmy thinks it is a long way from home, but he packs his clothes and travels to Marne to minister to his congregation.

Marne Methodist Church

Things do not go well. Maybe if he wasn't so far from home. Maybe if he hadn't "lost his faith" in college. Maybe.

He lives in the big white parsonage next to the church. The house is too big for one lonely young man. No one calls him Jimmy. He has been Jimmy all of his life, but now he is James, occasionally Jim. He is lonely and very homesick. He wants to be back on his streets, wants to go fishing with his dad and eat one of his Ma's good meals.

The young boy who never wanted anything to do with liquor, who always avoided the stuff, begins to drink. A lot. At first it is just beer, but it is not long before he graduates to the harder stuff. The bottles pile up behind the parsonage, Jimmy stuffs them in the trash and carries them to the dump.

Drinking turns out to be the least of his problems. He meets a young woman, a mother with three little children. She is the wife of one of the deacons in the church. Jimmy and the woman have an affair, an affair that lasts for months. No one finds out, but Jimmy is so scared, and feels so guilty, he finally can't take it. He resigns, returns to Hamilton and decides to look into another line of work. His sister, Faye, encourages him to get a teaching certificate and become a teacher.

Jimmy begins his teaching career in the little town of Marysville. Marysville is close to Hamilton, so close Jimmy can walk back and forth to school. He is no longer lonely; he likes the children and enjoys teaching. The children call him Mister Paulding but when he goes home and walks through Hamilton, people still call him Jimmy.

He does his best to forget Marne, to forget the woman, forget the liquor and the terrible homesickness that threatened to destroy him.

Ida has a hard time understanding. *Why isn't Jimmy preaching, why is he teaching in Marysville?* Jimmy confides in Faye, tells her about the drinking and the affair with the woman. Faye talks to Ida and convinces her that this is a better life for Jimmy.

JIMMY'S TRUE LOVE

The summer after Jimmy returns home from Marne, a new family moves in across the alley from the Paulding home. When Jimmy sees a young girl outside washing the family's very old car. he tells his brother, Tudie, that he is going to go ask that girl for a date. Tudie grins, *"She'll just say no, Jimmy."*

Thelma Agan in Hamilton

Jimmy ignores Tudie, walks across the alley and asks the young woman with the long red hair for a date. Tudie is right, she just says no. When Jimmy gets back, he tells Tudie that he is glad she said no, that she has more freckles than anyone he has ever seen.

That night when Jimmy walks down the sidewalk to go to church, the beautiful young woman with the long red hair catches up to him, slips her hand in his, and never lets go. The beautiful young woman is Thelma Agan.

Jimmy and Thelma spend all of their free time together. They are both teachers, so when school is out, they have many hours of freedom. Jimmy spends so much time at Thelma's house that her dad, George, threatens to throw him out. It is an idle threat. Thelma's entire family, including George, is crazy about Jimmy Paulding.

Three years after they meet, Jimmy and Thelma are married. They buy a little house in Hamilton, an old camp house called the Little Black House. The Little Black House is right next to

Uncle Shorty and Aunt Ruth's place, just down the block from Jimmy's childhood home. The Little Black House costs two hundred dollars and is completely furnished, including dishes, silverware, towels and bedding.

Jim and Thelma with Baby Jimmy

When the babies arrive, Aunt Ruth comes and helps Thelma for a few days. She baths the babies, holds them sweetly, remembering another little baby, remembering Baby. The first two children, Jimmy and Barbara, are both born at home in the Little Black House. Tommy, the youngest child, is born in the Knoxville hospital. After a week he comes home to Hamilton.

Jim, Thelma, Barbara and Jimmy

When the babies come, Thelma quits teaching and stays home to care for her children. Jimmy continues to teach. He seems to have found his real calling in life. He is a very good teacher and decides to become an administrator. Jimmy goes to Drake University and gets his Master's Degree in Education.

Superintendents seem to move around a lot. The family lives in many different little Iowa towns. Wherever they are, Jimmy and Thelma do their best to make a home for their children.

Even though Jimmy is a school superintendent, he is sometimes asked to preach in some of the local, rural churches. Jimmy seems to enjoy this type of ministry. He likes to see Thelma and his children sitting proudly in church.

It is a full life, mostly a life of love. Jimmy and Thelma never argue, at least not in front of the children. Maybe they both saw too much of that when they were growing up. They face their share of challenges, but they remain in love throughout their seventy-four years of marriage.

Jim and Thelma in Deep River

Jim and Thelma on their 60th wedding anniversary

EPILOGUE

My mother died when she was ninety-four years old. My father lived for another four years. During that time he lived at Northridge, an assisted living facility in Chariton, Iowa. Shortly after Mother died, Dad told me the story of Marne, about the drinking and the affair he had with the young mother. He seemed to feel very guilty about it. I told him these things happen, that people fall in love even when they probably shouldn't. That was the end of the initial conversation, but Dad continued to bring Marne up over the next few years.

Dad loved living at Northridge, loved the staff and other residents. Unfortunately after he had been living there for three and a half years, his money ran out. My husband and I brought him home to live with us.

Dad had been living with us for about three months when he called me into his room one morning. He sat up in bed and said, *"I'm worried about the boy."*

I assumed he was talking about one of my brothers, so I assured him that Jimmy and Tommy were fine. I told him that we could call them if he wanted to check it out for himself. He shook his head, said *"No, no, not Jimmy or Tommy. I'm worried about the baby, the baby boy in Marne."*

That is when I finally heard "The Rest Of The Story." Dad told me that the woman he had an affair with in Marne, when he was a young preacher, had gotten pregnant. He said that the baby was his. The baby was a little boy, a little boy that he was worried about, had been worried about for years. Dad told me that when he left Marne and went home, the woman came to Hamilton many times and tried to get him to leave with her. She wanted to divorce her husband. When she came to Hamilton, she always brought the baby with her. Dad's sister, Faye, took care of the baby so she and Dad could talk. Dad kept telling her it was over, that she should not divorce her husband. Then he met my mother. He didn't tell my mother about Marne, about the woman, or about his baby.

One of the last times the young woman from Marne came to Hamilton to see Dad, he tried once again to convince her that it was over, that she should stay with her husband. Dad doesn't remember when the woman finally gave up. He thinks that the last time he saw her and the baby was when he met her in Albia and told her that he planned to marry my mother, Thelma. The baby was about a year old the last time Dad saw him.

So that is the story of Marne. I was seventy-three years old when I found out that I had a half-brother someplace, a brother whose name I do not know.

Two months later, just before his 101 birthday, Dad had a heart attack and was taken to the Lucas County Hospital. Things seemed to be going pretty well until he had a second, massive heart attack. Just before he lost consciousness, he looked at me with those blue, blue Paulding eyes and asked me if I knew about Marne. I told him I knew all about it, that I knew about the boy and that

God had forgiven him for all of that a long, long time ago. Those are the last words I ever heard my father say.

On March eleventh, he opened his eyes for the first time in three days, looked up at seemingly nothingness, and died.

Rest in peace, Dad. Thanks for the memories.

APPENDIX

PAULDING ARCHIVES

Susan Knipe (Jacob's Mother)

Jacob Paulding

George Washington Wineland (Nancy's Father)

Nancy Wineland Paulding (Jacob's Wife)

Jacob and Nancy Paulding in Saint David, Illinois

VETERAN OF CIVIL WAR ANSWERS TAPS

(Central Press)

Jacob Paulding, St. David, Served Three Years with Indiana Regiment

Taps were sounded early today for Jacob Paulding, third oldest Civil war veteran in the county and the only one who resided in St. David. Death came at 2:30 a. m. at his home, where he had been bedfast for three months as the result of the infirmities of old age.

Mr. Paulding was approaching his ninety-fourth birthday anniversary. The only older Civil war veterans in this county are C. R. Sparger and E. Strube, both of Canton.

Mr. Paulding enlisted June 10, 1861, in Wabash county, Ind., his birthplace, serving three years with Co. A, 15th Ind. Vol. Inf. He was mustered out of service June 20, 1864.

His death leaves only 11 veterans of the Civil war remaining in this county. Five of them reside in Canton.

In St. David 44 Years

Born Feb. 25, 1841, a son of Curtis and Susan (Knipe) Paulding, he was married 70 years ago to Nellie Wineland, who died Jan. 29, 1929. Mr. Paulding made his home in St. David for 44 years.

Surviving children are Mrs. M. P. Smeltzer, St. David; Mrs. Susan Baxter, Knoxville, and John and Audrey Paulding, both of Hamilton, Iowa. Twenty grandchildren, 34 great-grandchildren, and one great-great-grandchild are also living.

Mr. Paulding, a coal miner by occupation, was a member of the Progressive Miners of America.

Funeral services will be held at 2:30 o'clock Sunday afternoon at the St. David Methodist Protestant church, with burial in Bryant cemetery. G. A. R. memorial services will be exemplified.

The flag at the G. A. R. hall was at half mast today out of respect to Mr. Paulding.

Jacob Paulding's Obituary

John Paulding's Draft Card

73

Paulding Family 1907

McCLURE ARCHIVES

ABRAHAM McCLURE

In memory of Brother Abraham McClure, who was born in Washington county, Virginia, about the year 1842; died at the home of his daughter, Mrs. McNew, near Simmons, Mo. April 18, 1919, making his age at death about 77 years. Was married to Mrs. Jane Ray in the year 186_. To this union were born five children, four girls and one boy, all of whom, with the aged widow, are yet living to mourn their loss, of a kind and loving husband and father. He was converted and united with the Methodist church at the age of 18 years and lived a true christian the rest of his life. Was a member of Elk Creek church at the time of his death. A good man in every way, as the writer has known him personally for about 45 years. The funeral was conducted by the undersigned at Oak Dale church April 19 and the body was laid to rest in Oak Dale cemetery to await the resurrection of the just. May God comfort and bless the sorrowing relatives.

J. J. C. TY.

CARD OF THANKS.

We wish to thank the neighbors and friends for their kindness and assistance shown during the sickness and after the death of our husband and father, Abe McClure. May God's richest blessings be with all such good friends.

MRS. JANE McCLURE.
MRS. M. B. McNEW.
MRS. IDA PAULDING.
MRS. M. E. BRATCHER.
MRS. ELIZA HOLT.
MR. J. S. McCLURE.

100 YEARS OLD

Mrs. Jane McClure of Simmons, Mo., grandmother of Mrs. J. T. Bausell of Lebanon, Va., celebrated her 100th birthday on February 5. Mrs. McClure was born at Willis, S. Ings, in the Moccasin section of Russell county, the daughter of Mr. and Mrs. Elisha Price.

Abraham McClure (Jimmy's Grandfather) Obituary & Card of Thanks
100ᵗʰ Birthday Notice of Biddy (Jimmy's Grandmother McClure)

Biddy's (Grandma McClure) 100th Birthday Party

Biddy & her daughter, Suze

MATILDA JANE McCLURE DEAD
OLDEST TEXAS CO. RESIDENT

Matilda Jane Price was born in Russell County, Virginia, February 5, 1840. Died at her home five miles south of Houston at 12:45 Sunday morning, July 21, 1940, making her age one hundred years, five months, and sixteen days.

She had been married twice. Stephen Ray was the first husband and one son of this marriage survives at the age of 78. Later she married Abraham McClure. They came to Texas County in 1892, locating near Tyrone, making their home there and on Elk Creek until Mr. McClure died in April, 1919. Since that time the aged lady has resided with her daughter, Mrs. Walters.

Surviving children from the second marriage are, Mrs. Martha Walters, Simmons, Mo.; James S. McClure, Stockton, Mo.; Mrs. Eliza Holt, of Virginia; Mrs. Ida Paulding, Hamilton, Iowa. She had 32 living grand children, 100 great grand children and several great great grand children. Grandchildren living in Texas County are the McNew brothers and Mrs. Dora Hinkle.

Mrs. McClure was born during the administration of Martin Van Buren. At her birth the Mexican war had not yet begun. Indians were very numerous and were exceedingly hostile. She told of one thrilling event. She and an aunt were milking, when they saw Indians approaching. Mrs. McClure, then Jane Price, managed to run to a hiding place, but her aunt was killed. The Indians then crowded into the house with wild yells and dances.

She underwent many hardships. Her mother died when she was nine years old and her father died when she was fifteen. She worked hard to help support her five brothers and one sister.

Mrs. McClure had been bedfast for about six months. She was always cheerful and was tenderly cared for by her daughters and other relatives.

Burial was at Oak Dale church Sunday afternoon, conducted by Rev. J. J. Carty. Music was furnished by Oak Dale choir with a special duet by Mrs. Rose Martin and Murrill Martin. Pall bearers were great grandsons, Ralph, Roy, Karl and Bill McNew, Lester and Chester Davis. Flower girls were great grand-daughters, Elma Hinkle, Neoma Davis, Loraine, Gynetha, Arlene and Jessie McNew. Services in charge of Elliott Funeral Directors.

A large circle of friends express their regret at the passing of this dear old lady, the oldest citizen in Texas County, and with a life record excelled by no one.

Card of Thanks

We wish to thank the friends and neighbors for their kindness and sympathy during the sickness and after the death of our mother and grand-mother, Mrs. Jane McClure.

Especially Rev. O. C. Stapleton for the prayer in the home and his comforting words; Rev. J. J. Carty for the consoling services at the church; for the beautiful songs and many floral offerings. May God richly bless each and every one is the earnest and sincere prayer of her children and grand children.

Biddy's Obituary

Ida's sister, Ever, & husband, Mr. Ward

Ida's sister, Ever McClure

Eliza McClure and "Sis" (Ida's sisters)

Martha B. McClure "Suze" (Ida's sister)

The Lord is my Shepherd; I shall not want. He maketh me to lie down in green pastures; He leadeth me beside the still waters. He restoreth my soul; He leadeth me in the paths of righteousness for His name's sake.

Yea, though I walk through the valley of the shadow of death, I will fear no evil; for Thou art with me; Thy rod and Thy staff they comfort me; Thou preparest a table before me in the presence of mine enemies; Thou anointest my head with oil, my cup runneth over.

Surely goodness and mercy shall follow me all the days of my life; and I will dwell in the house of the Lord forever.

IDA R. PAULDING

BORN
August 17, 1879
Russell County, Virginia

PASSED AWAY
July 16, 1975
Knoxville, Iowa

SERVICES
1 P.M., July 19, 1975
Hamilton Methodist Church

CLERGYMAN
Rev. Donald Otto

MUSIC
Soloist: Preshia Paulding
Pianist: Kenneth Paulding

BEARERS
Junior Pottorff   John McCombs
James Paulding
Robert Wallace   Steven McCombs
Pierce Godfrey

INTERMENT
Hamilton Cemetery

ARRANGEMENTS BY
Zimmerman Funeral Home
Lovilia, Iowa

Ida's Obituary

Thank you for reading!

Dear Reader,

I hope you enjoyed reading Stories From My Father. This book was originally intended for family members, but so many people requested copies I decided to make it available to a wider audience.

I learned so much from writing about the life of Jimmy Paulding, things that have helped me understand more about my own life's journey. I now know that even the most honorable of men can have closely held secrets that weigh upon their hearts and worry them, right up until the day they die. I think that is part of being human.

I love to hear from readers, so please share your thoughts about this book with me. You can write to me at barbpaulding@gmail.com.

Finally, I'd like to ask you for a favor. If you're willing, I'd love a review of Stories From My Father. I would enjoy getting your feedback. Reviews can be tough to come by. You, as the reader and reviewer, can make or break a book. So, if you have the time, I'd appreciate a review on Amazon.

I hope you enjoyed meeting Jimmy Paulding and sharing in his life's journey. He was a great storyteller, educator, and man.

Thank you so much for reading Stories From My Father.

With heartfelt thanks,

Barbara Paulding

ABOUT THE AUTHOR

Barbara was born in Hamilton, Iowa in "The Little Black House," a coal miner's shack covered in tarpaper. Her grandparents, aunts, uncles and cousins all lived within a few blocks of her home. All of the men in her family worked in the mines at some point in their lives. Barbara remembers seeing them come home at night, covered in coal dust, only their eyes and white teeth shining through the dirt.

When Barbara was seventeen, she left the coal mining towns of southern Iowa to attend the University of Iowa, where she earned her BA and MA in psychology.

Barbara has returned to her roots and now lives with her husband, Kirk Moody, on a small acreage in southern Iowa. She has written a novel, *Ghost Town Truck Stop*.

www.ingramcontent.com/pod-product-compliance
Lightning Source LLC
Chambersburg PA
CBHW081220020426
42331CB00012B/3056